Our Issues His Virtue

The Benefits of Laying Our Issues at the Feet of Jesus.

Compiled By
Tawanda M. Schultz

Edited by: Claude R. Royston

BK Royston Publishing, LLC
Jeffersonville, IN

BK Royston Publishing
P. O. Box 4321
Jeffersonville, IN 47131
502-802-5385
http://bkroystonpublishing.com
bkroystonpublishing@gmail.com

© Copyright – 2015

All Rights Reserved. No part of this book may be reproduced, stored in a retrieval system, or transmitted by any means without the written permission of the author.

Published by: BK Royston Publishing LLC
Cover Design: Customweb.com
Logo Design and Development: Christopher Martin
Layout: BK Royston Publishing LLC

ISBN-13: 978-0692510353
ISBN-10: 0692510354
LCCN: 2015913294

Printed in the United States of America

Dedication

To my daughter, Kaisey. When I look at you, I realize everything that my mother, grandmothers, and aunts have all endeavored to teach me. They displayed their love for me through loving and sometimes harsh or stern words, acts of kindness, care taking, sacrifices, tears and prayers. I didn't always understand until you came into my life. Now I know that all that they had done was to let me know, which I am now telling you that you are beautiful and blessed of the Lord. You are a precious and rare jewel. You are fearfully and wonderfully made. God entrusted you to my care and I will honor Him by loving you as long as I live. I want you to understand that we as women will all endure some sort of labor in life. We all have issues. We carry our issues differently than men do because…well, we are women (smile). We are emotional beings. Many of us go through the same or similar issues. Remember, you are not alone. There will always be someone who has experienced something similar to what you go through. Also remember to be a witness to others what God has done for you and how he can do the same for them. I'm so glad that you are a remarkable woman of God. I am so glad that God allowed me to be your mom.

Acknowledgements

The creation of this anthology would not have been made possible without the women who contributed. These women devoted their time and their treasured testimonies. I would be remiss if I did not take out the time to acknowledge each of you. It took a lot of prayer and patience in order for this vision to come together. This was neither a simple nor an easy task. You had to dig deep down in your soul and allow God to draw from you some of your inner most secret issues to be put on display for so many to see. However the purpose was greater than that. You have allowed yourself to be used by God to be a testimony and a witness for Christ. There is someone that is going to read your story and begin their journey of healing, faith in God, hope, freedom and victory. I know each of you, some our paths crossed simply for this purpose and some I have known a little longer and a little more intimately. However we met, it was by divine order. I know without the shadow of a doubt that you have confessed the Lord Jesus Christ as your personal savior and by doing so you have said to the Lord one or all of these phrases; use me, send me, speak through me, not my will but thine be done. Well this book of testimonies is an example of your selfless confession to Jesus Christ and your commitment to building the kingdom of God. We need it today, now more than ever.

So with a grateful heart, I say to you. Thank you for allowing yourself to be used and thank you for helping me to allow God to use me. Again, I **could not** have done this without you. And, congratulations! You are the first authors in volume one of *'Our Issues, His Virtue'*, *The Benefits of Laying Our Issues at the Feet of Jesus Christ.*

Fleur S. Van Pelt

Mya Byrd

Barbara Archer

Sulena Morris-Breland

Camille Perry

Gina Edwards

Sonja Hubbard

Joyce Schultz

Charmagne R. Quarles

Kellye Hubbard

Faye Mosby

Lorraine Dryden

Esther Graham

Julia A. Royston

Tawanda M. Schultz

Introduction

As women, we have all had to endure some sort of problems in our lives. We have gone through numerous trials and tribulations, and we have felt completely alone. The truth is, we are not alone because someone has experienced similar situations and shared experiences. From the days of Genesis until present day, until the end of time as we know it, women have had to and will continue to deal with issues of life. Many women have been overwhelmed with abuse, afflictions, and self-doubt. Other women have been overcome with grief, sickness, and abandonment while others have had to deal with brokenness, adultery, and barrenness. Women have experienced loneliness and have had the unthinkable happen. These are just some issues that women from all walks of life and through-out the world have had to endure. Like Sarah, some lacked faith and patience and became presumptuous and got ahead of God. Some, like Hagar have been used, abused and abandoned. Others like the woman at the well, have had many lovers. Others like Mary, have found themselves ashamed because they found themselves unmarried and with child. The woman with the issue of blood needed a healing from the Lord. We, like her, have to learn that we have been given the power to receive healing of all of our issues from virtue of Jesus. Remember the woman with the blood issue had no one else to turn to. Notice her circumstances, she was plagued with hemorrhaging and had spent all her money on doctors who could not help her. She was isolated and her back was against the wall. She had no money and no hope. However, she decided that she would not allow her circumstances to define her. She would not accept the life sentence that was given to her. She was not content with living condemned. She decided to get up and receive her healing from the Lord Jesus (Matthew 9:20 KJV).

The women who you will encounter in the pages of this book believed, like the many women of the bible, that they could receive their resolve by way of the virtue of God through Jesus Christ. They believed that God's virtue could and would deliver and/or heal them of their various issues. They depended on and trusted Jesus, the one who is the answer to all of life's issues, the true savior. As you-read through the pages of this book, you will meet women who have decided to share with you some of their own personal issues. Some are completely transparent because they believe <u>God's word where He says</u>, 'And they overcome him by the blood of the lamb and the word of your testimony....' Rev 12:11 KJV They have decided to encourage you so that you know that you are not alone and that God is a promise keeper. Others offer words of encouragement in hopes that you will keep your eyes on Jesus while you are going through whatever your issue may be or simply to forgive yourself for what you may have done. If you would just put your faith and trust in Him, by His virtue, He will see you through. The reason I decided to compile this book of testimonies is because God gave me a vision of women being set free from the bondage and shame of their past or current situation. I know someone reading this feels like there is no hope. I know there are women who can't get away from their own thoughts and feeling of condemnation and unforgiveness. There are women reading this who feel as though no one loves them and they are alone. Again, I say to you, you are not alone. Jesus loves you and He wants you to know that He has come to set you free.

And for those of you who have just come by to be spectators, God has a plan and a promise for you too.

Table of Contents

Acknowledgements
Introduction

I'm Proud of My Shame Fleur S. Van Pelt	1
When God Says Move... You Move Mya Byrd	7
Breaking Free of Insanity Barbara Archer	19
Verse Now in the Song of My Life Sulena Morris-Breland	29
His Grace Kept Me Camille Perry	33
Daddy's Little Girl! Gina Edwards	43
I'll Fix It! Sonja Hubbard	51
My Jehovah Rapha Joyce Schultz	63

Finding the God in Me   69
Charmagne R. Quarles

I'm More Than My Failures   81
Kellye Hubbard

The Wait   95
Faye Mosby

Destiny Child   107
Lorraine Dryden

A New Heart   121
Esther Graham

The Least Likely but Through God I Did   127
Julia A. Royston

What's Love Got to Do With It?   133
Tawanda M. Schultz

"There is therefore now no condemnation to them which are in Christ Jesus, who walk not after the flesh, but after the Spirit." Romans 8:1

I'm Proud of My Shame!

Wait, what?!

Yes, I'm proud of my shame. Because my shame, which is another word for my past, has taught me three very important truths that changed my life. Allow me to share with you!

Truth # 3.

I know that I am set free. And my gracious, what a sweet freedom it is. God has forgiven me of everything. And I do mean everything. He has promised me that he has placed my sins as far as the East is from the West, and He will remember them no more. I NEED this from God. We all need this from God. He knows us thoroughly, with Him we are fully exposed. What did He forgive you of? Some of us were occult members, some thieves, or prostitutes. Some were skilled liars and artful deceivers. Others were addicted to drugs, or full of rage and hate. And still there are some that were all of these things.... I am so thankful that the shed blood of Jesus Christ cleanses from ALL unrighteousness, and that I, Thank God, won't have to explain why I was so wretched. Oh I thank God for showing me this. My past is dead to Him. As the hymn says, "Amazing Grace how sweet the sound, that saved a wretch like me." 1 John 1:9, Psalm 103:11-12, Hebrews 8:12

Truth #2

I know how to empathize with others. And people need empathy. One never knows what another human being has been through. Aren't there things in your life that you would never share, under any circumstance? It's reasonable to assume that if you have deep secrets, then your neighbor, cousin, choir director, and friends must have them too. I have learned to be soft hearted and kind, so that I can recognize when the Holy Spirit is prompting me towards a healing word of encouragement. People are filled with hurt and bitterness, and they are lost and looking for anything to guide them. God can use our past to help someone going through that very same thing. But if I am too busy looking down on, surmising and assuming about someone, then I cannot be used by God to help them. We must have pity, be merciful and kind. We must remember that, "There, but for the Grace of God, go I". Luke 6:36, Ephesians 4:32

Truth #1

I have learned to love God more deeply. As I mentioned before, God has forgiven me of so much. While I was yet a sinner, Christ died for me. And He has made plans for my life. Plans to prosper me and to give me health. He has ordered my steps, and is a Light and Comforter. He has only my best interest at heart. He wants to use me for His Kingdom. I don't have to lament my shame, my past, because, despite all of my shortcomings, God lifted my head. How can I help but love Him? And He is no respecter of persons. These three truths are pertinent to all of us who confess Jesus Christ is Lord. Praise God that "Christ has regarded my helpless estate, and has shed His own blood for my soul!" Jeremiah 29:11, Psalm 3:3, Psalm 37:23, Acts 10:34

That is why I am proud of my shame. It does not hold me down, because I am forgiven. It does not hurt me, because I use it to help others. It does not dictate my future, because I know who definitely holds that. .

Fleur S. VanPelt
Artist
Slidell, LA

"Thus says the Lord, who makes a way in the sea, a path in the mighty waters, who brings forth chariot and horse, army and warrior; they lie down, they cannot rise, they are extinguished, quenched like a wick: Remember not the former things, nor consider the things of old. Behold, I am doing a new thing; now it springs forth, do you not perceive it? I will make a way in the wilderness and rivers in the desert. The wild beasts will honor me, the jackals and the ostriches, for I give water in the wilderness, rivers in the desert, to give drink to my chosen people, the people whom I formed for myself that they might declare my praise."

Isaiah 43: 16-21

When God Says Move...You Move!

January 1, 2011

I married the father of my child and the love of my life. His dream, we would move to Dallas, TX and live happily ever after...my dream, to just live happily ever after.

My husband proudly announced to all of his friends and family that we were moving to Dallas, after all, it was something he always wanted to do and it felt like, "home" to him. We tried to move, but nothing worked out, he was self-employed and would have to build his business, I couldn't find a job, we couldn't find a place to live. Nothing and I mean nothing, worked! I finally told him, it wasn't time, that didn't mean that we would never move, it just meant not yet. We needed to wait on God's timing. He told me, that I could wait on God's timing, but, he would be gone. He was upset, blamed me and decided that it was my fault his dream wouldn't come true.

September 3, 2012

The vacation was now over and it was time to head back to reality. We now had two little girls, misery, unfulfilled dreams, and a marriage that was filled with chaos and headed for destruction. I prayed prior to this trip that God would mark this time as the beginning of the turning point in our marriage. I never imagined what the outcome of my prayer would look like.

The arguments got so bad this time, that when we got on the plane, he sat in one part and I in the other. When we landed, he got a ride and went in one direction and I the other. By the time I got home, he was moving his things out and leaving. At this moment, something in me knew that he would NEVER come back to this house.

September 4, 2012

I have to find a job! My baby was 6 months old, the plan was that I would stay home with her until she turned 1, just as I had done with my oldest daughter. But, the plan was aborted at this point, my husband was gone and I needed a job so that I could support myself and my two children.

Finding a job was always easy for me, after all, I had a MBA, a wonderful resume and a superb recruiter. This time was different, my recruiter was confused, he was not getting any hits on my resume at all and a task that was always easy had turned impossible!

September 21, 2012

My friend who was in HR at a major corporation in St. Louis called me. She had a position for me! All I had to do was contact her in the morning for a phone interview, come in for a face to face interview with her and then after that, I would be her top candidate and the job would be mine! Thank you Jesus!

My best friend and I were on the phone talking that evening, she had moved out of St. Louis 3 years prior to this, and although she and I never really had this conversation before, she was really persistent in saying that we should move out of St. Louis. She told me that moving her son away from STL was the best thing she could've ever done and that it was no place for a black man. I quickly told her that I was not a black man, I had no desire to move and that was the end of that. She wouldn't let it go, she persisted. So, to make her be quiet, I simply told her that right now, I was going to work this job and that if God wanted me to move, he would make it so that I didn't get it.

My focus was working and taking care of my children, not moving anywhere!

September 24, 2012

My HR friend called, she was in a panic. The job that was "mine" had been snatched away! The CEO's daughter called and decided that the job would be a perfect match for a friend of hers. The friend started immediately. My friend assured me not to worry; she would find me a new job. I simply laughed and told her I understood and it was ok!

I contacted my best friend, informed her that I wasn't going to get the job so I needed to figure something else out. She was excited, and said, "Mya, I thought that whether or not you got the job would be the determining factor of whether or not you would move!" I told her, "Girl please, I'm NOT moving! I only said that so you would be quiet! Again, she insisted that moving was what was needed and that we should move. So, again, to make her get off my back, I simply told her, if God wants us to move, then he would place it upon my husband's heart to say the word, "Texas" to me.

September 29, 2012

My husband was over at the house visiting when he remembered something that he forgot to tell me. He told me that a mutual friend of ours went to visit his brother who had moved to Phoenix, on his way back, he got locked up in…..(you guessed it), "TEXAS!" I was washing dishes at the time, I turned and looked at him and said, "He what?" Again, my husband stated, yeah, he got locked up in Texas! I went through who, what, when, where and how. I couldn't believe he was saying this word! Finally, he asked me what was wrong with me, why did I keep asking him all these questions…I started to sob and exclaimed, "No, No, No, you don't understand! You were NOT supposed to say that word!" He asked, "What word?" I exclaimed, "Texas!"

At this moment, I began to explain to my husband what had occurred up to this point; he simply looked at me and said, "That's just a coincidence!" I told him, there is no such thing as a "coincidence".

For the first time ever, we had a real heart to heart talk. My husband explained to me that when I didn't go along with his dream to move to Texas, he equated that to when he was 16 years old and his father told him to save up money and he would help him buy a new car. He saved the money and when it was time to buy the car, his father backed out.

He also equated it to when he asked his father to help him pay for college and he told him no. My husband told me that I was the one person he thought would never let him down and when I did, he checked out and decided he did not want to be married anymore. He told me that he had told someone else that if we didn't move to Dallas, then our marriage would never work. I was dumbfounded. I knew that he really wanted to move, but I didn't realize it was this important to him. I also never realized that his expectation for me was so great! I asked him why he never shared any of this with me before, he simply stated, you never listened.

That night, I prayed hard, I told God that I needed to know if this was Him, if this was truly Him showing me that we needed to move. I told him that I needed Him to do for me what He had done for Gideon. I needed a third sign! If this was truly Him, I needed him to create a job for me in Texas. As soon as I finished praying I got up and applied for multiple jobs in Dallas and then went to bed.

October 1, 2012

My phone rang off the hook all day, job after job, recruiter after recruiter. One job wanted me to start working that Friday. This was becoming a reality; I would have to move to Texas! I slowly began to accept the idea; I arranged the interviews and told the recruiters I would inform them as soon as I arrived. I planned to move right after Thanksgiving, but I never had any peace in deciding to procrastinate.

I began to read scripture after scripture and listen to sermon after sermon; everyone was saying the same thing. When God says move, you move now! If you procrastinate, it's the same thing as disobedience. When God told Abraham to sacrifice Isaac, he got up the next morning and went to do it!

I realized my procrastination was because I didn't really want to go, however, I wanted to be obedient. So I prayed, I told the Lord, that I had made a commitment to Him and the women in the class that I was teaching at the time. But, if he allowed me to finish teaching His daughters, as soon as the class ended, I would move! Only one dilemma, how would I tell my mother and grandmother?

Before when we were talking about moving, my mother cried and was very upset, my grandmother was upset and called my husband's grandmother and touched and agreed that they would pray against us going. So, how was I going to explain all of this to them???

October 11, 2012

A recruiter called me from one of the companies I applied to, he was impressed by my resume and wanted to speak with my references. My mom happened to be one of my references. Oh my God, I would have to tell her prior to him calling.

I informed my mom that a recruiter would be calling her, she was excited! "From where Mya?" I froze up, I couldn't tell her...her voice lowered, "Mya....are you all moving to Texas?" I quickly got upset, "Why would you say I thing like that? What would make you think we would be moving to Texas?"

My mom said, "The other day, I was walking down the stairs in my house and I heard in my spirit, "Mya and her husband are going to get back together, but, they will be moving to Texas." She said, when I heard this, I said out loud, "No, they can't move to Texas, I can't afford to go back and forth there." She then heard, "the money you use to help pay for your granddaughter's tuition, you can use to pay for your flights." At this moment she had peace and went about her day and totally forgot to tell me about her experience. I was in total awe and full of praise! The Lord had given me the same favor that he did for Gideon. Not only did he provide me with the 3 signs I asked for, He gave me a 4th that I didn't ask for just to let me know it was definitely Him! While I was trying to figure it out, God WORKED IT OUT!!!!!

It was a reality, I was afraid, but I was excited to see what My Father had in store for me! I didn't allow my fear to paralyze me. One night, when I awoke in the middle of the night, I heard Joyce Meyers preach a sermon, "Go Afraid". That became my motto, I was going afraid. The Lord gave me unthinkable favor everywhere I turned, from obtaining the moving truck to renting my house out, to getting us a place to stay in the interim. My class ended October 22nd and on October 25th, we were on the highway headed for our new home...Dallas, Texas! When God said, "MOVE", I MOVED and as a result, so many doors have been opened so many blessings have come down, that I KNOW without a shadow of a doubt would've never taken place had I not been obedient. I won't lie and tell you that I didn't have to go through a wilderness season, I did. Whenever God takes you to the land of milk and honey, you must first pass the tests and go through your wilderness season. God is FAITHFUL and every day that I awake in my new home in Dallas...I can do nothing but give Him all the praises, honor and glory!!!!!!! Hallelujah!!!

Mya Byrd, MBA
Tax Professional
Ft. Worth, TX

"So do not throw away your confidence it will be richly rewarded you need to preserve so that when you have done the will of God you will receive what he has promised."

Hebrews 10: 35-36

Breaking Free of Insanity

Most of us live a life of insanity but we are not aware that our lives have spun out of control. What is the definition of insanity? Doing the same thing over and over and expecting a different result. That was my story, but I know I am not by myself. If you find yourself here take heart. You are in good company. For years I wondered why my life was so crazy. Deep down I desired a better way of life, but had no idea how to obtain it. Does that sound familiar to you? Even after I gave my heart to the Lord, I thought now I will have a different life. The only problem with that thinking is I never released everything into God's capable hands. Allow me to take you on a journey of my life and how God stepped in after thirty-two years and gave me an expiration date of my insanity.

As a young child I grew up with a very dysfunctional father who introduced me to a life of infidelity at the age of 7. My father was always the ladies' man and the women were always attracted to him. As I look back, I knew it was wrong, but I never mentioned anything to my mother. It was as though I knew the importance of keeping my mouth shut. My mother was a Christian woman who raised us in church and taught us about God, I often wondered "how a great woman like my mother ended up with a man like my father," I guess love is blind. I would see my father go away for the weekends and it was not work related. I knew he was going away with other women and so did my mother, she simply did not care. My mother probably thought while he is gone it will be quiet in the house and it was. There was no yelling involved. Mom would always take us out when our father would leave. We always enjoyed our weekends until one Friday night when my father assaulted my mother. That was the last straw. My mother began to execute her plan for leaving him. She had endured enough from him. We relocated to Frederick, Maryland where my mother grew up and life was good. My sister began to have outbursts all the time. Finally, my mother took her to the doctor and after a psychiatric evaluation it was determined that my father had molested her. At that time a lot made sense. My sister had anger towards my mother. She believed that my mother suspected something and did not protect her. I know what she means. As long as I could remember my mother never allowed my sister to stay home alone with my father. My mother had no problem with me and my other sister staying at home with my father but never my middle sister. As young children, we look to our parents to protect us and when our parents fail us, what is a child to do? Obviously the dysfunction ran further into my family tree than I ever expected. My sister's relationship with my mother was strained for years. After a few years had gone by I met a guy at the Frederick Fair. I had no idea at the time that my life would change for the worse. We began to date one another and my mother did not approve. The more she disapproved the more I was attracted to him. I started sneaking behind my mother's back to date him but one night all my mother's concerns came to pass. He raped me and left me alone, scared and nearly dead. That night my life changed and I was never the same again. What he stole from me I could never get back. I tried so many things to numb my pain such as drinking, playing hooky from school, smoking cigarettes and partying. My mother thought I was just acting out she never thought, 'could it be because of the rape?' So often she would get her sisters to come into town and gang up on me. I always referred to them as hound dogs. I can recall they would yell and tell me things like "you are nothing," "you are like your father" and "you will never be anything but a bum." Those words stayed with me my entire life. I never felt good about myself and always thought I was a failure. Words are very powerful and they stay with you forever, for me thirty-two years. I tried so often to try to push his hands off my body in my mind, but I was never successful at it. All I ever wanted was to be loved and have someone love me and yes, I did, however, meet someone real special named Larry and we got married. But even the marriage was not good. I struggled with intimacy and I had a hard time making love even on our wedding night. My new husband had to go for a drive in the car. That left me feeling alone and rejected once again. I felt like a failure. Those spoken words came rushing back to my mind. Months had passed, finally we were able to make love but even then it was not fully engaging but just enough for me to get pregnant. I knew I did not want to be a mother so I had an abortion. At the time I was almost five months pregnant. My husband was upset but I did not care. All I wanted was to be free. Within months I started having affairs behind my husband's back. Whenever I felt afraid I would spiral out of control and before long I began a life of committing crimes, which eventually landed me in prison. When I had my son I knew after I laid my eyes on him things had to change and it did for a while. A few years had passed and I had my daughter by a married man who lived across the hall from my apartment. My life was always out of control. I always wanted more and I was never satisfied. One thing for sure life will take you through many storms and if you are not careful, it will lead you down a path of destruction. That is what Satan does. So often things that happen to us might not manifest themselves until years later. He is a very patient person. He will wait. In my case that is what happened because I had a third child, I walked away from him and two days later I landed back in prison. I knew I had hit rock bottom when I could have a child and never really know what I had. But God had a plan and I gave my heart to Jesus March 27, 1997 at 5:10 p.m. on Thursday evening. I was released from prison to come home just in time before my children were handed over to a state program. It is ironic that I did not want the child I had and I almost lost my kids that I did want. I had a long battle with my court dates. I had over forty-two counts of theft during my insanity. I started hanging out with the wrong people and I began to hot wire cars and sell the parts. I finally began breaking into homes until we got caught by a neighbor, but nothing came from it. The reason there were no charges was because my girlfriend's boyfriend was a major drug dealer and he made sure she would not talk with the authorities. God brought me through all the charges and I was sentenced to one year of supervised probation and two years unsupervised probation. I thought now everything will be fine, but I soon found myself in another abusive relationship with a man I met at my church. We were married. Everything I went through with him took me right back to that little girl who was raped that night many years prior. I was never healed and restored from that night and as a result I made poor decisions. I went from one poor relationship to another. For years I wondered "will I ever find the right person?" I was that woman at the well whom Jesus met on his journey. I had many husbands and some were not mine. My life got worse than better, but I never dealt with the pain until years later when God stepped in and gave my insanity an expiration date July 2012. I lost everything, my third marriage, home, cars, and finally the job. I could not believe all this was happening. I found myself homeless along with my two children. Yes, God bankrupt me of everything, but God finally had all of me and not just part of me. I registered to an online bible study through Proverbs 31 Ministries. Through ministry, God began to bring some healing to my life. At my church I started to attend, "Celebrate Recovery," which is a ministry to help people deal with their issues. I was in a place I could no longer run. I had to face the reality that I had escaped for 32 years. God used that ministry to bring about complete healing and restoration. I had no idea that my soul was damaged and all the anger I had in my soul. Through it all, I finally began to see who I am and that God loves me with an everlasting love. Because of what Jesus did on the cross that makes me good. I am no longer defined by my past. I am victorious. I had no confidence in my abilities, but now I finally do. I have a holy confidence. Since then I wrote my book called "Tell All, From Insanity to Sane." I then started a business which I teach and minister to women who are struggling in their minds. I am living a life on purpose. My desire is to see every woman free in their minds, soul and body. We all have struggles in life from our past. When we make a conscious decision to not deal with our past there is a door for Satan to come in and lead us down a path of destruction. His sole purpose is for you to not know who you are and what you were created to be. The mind is the first place the enemy will attack. You must guard your mind and your thoughts. All those years the enemy was after my mind. If he can get your mind he will have you. My soul was damaged. Our souls are made up of Mind, Will and Emotions. Every decision I ever made in life resulted from all three areas. There were times I could not even settle my thoughts or emotions, but deep down I knew there had to be an opposite of this insanity and there was. You do not have to be a slave to your past. You can be free and live the life Christ died for you to experience. All my days I will continue to speak and educate women on transformation. You may be reading this and see a little of yourself in my story. It is alright, do not feel like no one will understand, that is simply not true. As women we wear many hats and masks, but you have to get to a place when you become real. If you cannot be real with yourself, you will never be real with God. I knew God had a deliverance for me and I wanted it more than anything else. My question to you is, "How desperate are you wanting freedom? " Free from all the wrong thinking and negative thoughts and all the past hurts, and pains. As you begin to walk out your purpose you will discover your purpose is in your pain. What God showed me was that the very thing that caused me the most grief is the exact thing God has used to bring about my deliverance. You too can be healed and delivered and set free so you can live the life of freedom. Last words: Remember, God loves you with an Everlasting Love.

Barbara Archer
Radio Show Host
Atlanta, GA

"A Psalm. O sing unto the LORD a new song; for he hath done marvelous things: his right hand and his holy arm, hath gotten him the victory."
Psalm 98:1

Verse Now in the Song of My Life

Preceded by verses of a mixture of joy and pain, triumph and defeat, positive and negative lyrics that could make some head scratch, give up and give in I stand.

 Girded with truth by his grace I'm grateful to not only live but am beginning again to receive his abundance and enjoy life.

Born and raised in Christianity I have the honor of Godly parents. Though not flawless they were certainly not faithless. My weeks were filled with church services and Christian activities that kept me out of trouble. However, not all of them taught me how to stay out of trouble! So as I aged and matured mentally and physically I sought the God of Christianity personally. I'll never forget the first time I heard the voice of the Father audibly! It was late afternoon in the school week. I was walking home from school and I heard the Father clearly say "I love you".

Listen when I tell you of the peace and assurance that flooded my soul in that moment! There's no better assurance than that of God's love for you! The love of another is an amenity and not a necessity. Because He loves me, I know how to love Him. Because He loves me, I'm empowered to love myself. Because He loves me I love others. Because He loves me....

With each day I learn Him more. Trials get easier, triumphs get sweeter. I've learned to live by faith and express His nature by glory!

Rev. Sulena Olivia Morris-Breland
Aberdeen, MD

"This I recall to my mind, therefore have I hope. 22 It is of the Lord's mercies that we are not consumed, because his compassions fail not. 23 They are new every morning: great is thy faithfulness."
Lamentations 3:21-23

His Grace Kept Me

During the preparation for this submission it seemed as though nothing I wanted to share would be fitting or that I didn't have enough or even the right words to say. But as time drew near I had to be honest with myself and see that it was simply an attack from the enemy in keeping me bound from expressing the joy and freedom God has given to me.

So here it is….

One of my favorite scriptures Lamentations 3:21-23, and the theme of my life; I was born on May 24th, 1984 to saved parents who taught my sister and I through words and deeds the importance of having a true and committed relationship with Christ. They instilled love, morals, values and the principles of being wholesome young ladies in this world. Growing up in a two-parent home where father brought home the bacon and was the king of the castle, while mother would turn simple ingredients to delicious meals and champion her husband every step of the way; you would think it would be rather strange that their daughter would suffer from depression, low self-esteem and anxiety. Why would she think less of herself? Why would she not see her own worth? How could she allow herself to get into these various relationships that were destined for catastrophe? Didn't her dad and mom teach her anything?

Well, the answer is yes! They did teach me but not all people who suffer from these life issues are caused by some sort of troubled past. The scripture states in John 10:10a that the thief cometh not, but for to steal, and to kill, and to destroy. He doesn't have a checklist of qualifications the individual must meet in order for him do to his plan; he just simply just does what comes natural to him. I can't really explain the first time I noticed that I thought less of myself or not worthy. Growing up kids tease and poke fun because that is what we do as children, I was always the tallest in my class even in kindergarten as my teacher Ms. Coleman was a midget. I have full lips that I used to get hassled about not to mention my skin color, since I was the only black girl in the class for many years. But that wasn't it, honestly God has given me such a quick-wit that when most people teased and made fun of me, I would fire back so quickly with such retorts and candor that people began to pick their words with me. I was always a little heavy. I loved to eat and food was fun! Cooking and baking were my after school hobbies when I decided to take a break from my Super Nintendo or Sega Genesis. Calorie counting wasn't even a thought during those years, so yes my body started to show forth the signs that I was eating too much. Now, being an oversized pre-teen in the 90s was not as common but I had a good defense mechanism…Comedy!

One night my father and I were sitting down to play dominoes and of course like normal we started playing the dozens with each other. I cracked on his Mac & Me like physique and he cracked on my large feet that I inherited from him. Then we took to pen and paper. I drew a stick figure with large head and feet with gigantic soup-coolers for lips. All laughs and giggles at this point, well then he had the nerve to draw something about me…..three circles one small-medium for my head, a larger circle for my body and two oddly shaped circles for my feet. Well the little sensitive and insecure young girl saw that drawing and just broke down and ran away. I was fifteen years old and I can still remember thinking to myself, "if my daddy sees me like this then what they say must be true!" (Now, before I go any further, by no means do I carry any anger or resentment towards my father. My dad truly is the best man I have ever known! I'm just giving you some context to where it all began.) My mom was in the kitchen and she heard my dramatic exit and says to my father, 'See this is why I never played the dozens, it never ends well for someone', she was sooooo right!

But it was that night that I just decided to say, "You know what I don't want to be fat anymore." Well, for the next six months I didn't eat, not fully starving myself but let's just say I went from 220lbs to 160lbs within that time. The weight seriously just fell off! I went from being the fluffy baby sister to this developed - curvy vivacious sixteen year old who was now turning the heads of the boys in school and around her neighborhood. The attention I received was night and day! I wasn't used to it. Guys were not trying to have me be their bestie or home-girl, they talked to me like a girl! And it went straight to my head! For over 7 years through the conclusion of high school to college I thrived off the attention I would get from men, not realizing that every guy I encountered was just a live example of how little I truly loved myself. So at 23 I had a mental and emotional breakdown, I was drinking a bottle of wine a night. People had no idea not even my family, I was working, going to school and lived on my own. In the eyes of many Camille was doing awesome! I knew how to put on the smile and grace to keep everyone in the dark. Well, you can't lie to God and He saw my brokenness and how reckless His child was being.

Now, mind you, I grew up in church, served in ministry, exhorted the people of God and sang with the praise team! I knew the scriptures and I would tell others how much God loved them. But when it came to applying it I failed miserably. I would be terrified to go to sleep thinking I wouldn't wake up and anxiety attacks were common daily occurrences. I saw therapists and I would tell them my story and they would laugh not at me but at my delivery they would say….so I got to the point of realizing you know what I refuse to tell anyone about this. And I heard a voice respond and say, 'Tell Me' so I did. I just started talking. Boy I tell you, I thought I was just gonna' talk the voice away. The more I talked the more He listened, and when it was time for me to sleep I could hear Him talk to me. He reminded me in His word in Psalm 139:14 I will praise thee; for I am fearfully and wonderfully made: marvelous are thy works; and that my soul knoweth right well. He would show me in His creation that He had plans for me and scriptures that talked about how He cares for the sparrows and how He clothes the fields and how He would take care of me.

I had to learn to apply the Word of God to my life, my shortcomings and insecurities. I had to understand who I was in Christ, I had to understand that God is forgiving and loving. In all of my errors in life He still poured out His mercy and grace on my life. The journey of life is truly one that is filled with turns and winding roads but just knowing that God is with me brings such comfort. I am on the eve of my 31st birthday and I look back to yesteryears of my life and I can see just how accurately the Prophet Jeremiah pinned

Lamentations 3:21-23, 21 This I recall to my mind, therefore have I hope. 22 It is of the Lord's mercies that we are not consumed, because his compassions fail not. 23 They are new every morning: great is thy faithfulness.

God didn't let me stay in the mess I was in, He didn't allow me to be cut down or succumb to the temptation of ending my own life. He gave me hope! He gave me peace!

The best part of John 10:10 is that even though you hear what the enemy's job is Christ simply interjects and throws what came before out of the window with, **"I am come that they might have life, and that they might have it more abundantly"**.

Now even though my body has gone through more changes I LOVE MYSELF! I look into the mirror and see God's jewel. It didn't happen overnight but with His help He has comforted me and shown me just who I am. And for that I am eternally grateful! I solicit to each and every one of you that may read this book, Trust God! Don't give up on God, no matter the situation He has come to give us LIFE and that More Abundantly!

Minister Camille Perry, MBA
Eastvale, Ca

And, "I will be a Father to you, and you will be my sons and daughters, says the Lord Almighty."

2 Corinthians 6:18

Daddy's Little Girl!

When I was born, I became Daddy's little girl instantly! After my parents had two boys I was told my father prayed for a little girl and nine months later, I arrived. So you know what that meant right; I got my way all of the time, I had my Dad's heart and wallet (smile) and I could do NO wrong in his eyes. This arrangement worked well for me, even as I became a young woman; because no one loved me like my Daddy! He was always there to talk to, I could rely on him and he took care of me like a princess! In fact, he was the first man to give me flowers and my first diamonds.

Oh, the talks we used to have; they were so engaging! Daddy – the Rev. Jay Crawley Randolph Edwards, was a Pastor and an intellect, so you have to be sharp to keep up with him. We would enjoy conversations around the Bible, philosophy, family and just plain life!

When he wasn't making you laugh, he was teaching you a profound truth!

I remember when I got my first apartment, he gave me a personalized "Dear Baby" note and a check to buy all of my groceries. I still have the note to this day! When I found out I was pregnant with my son, I was so scared and nervous to tell him. How do you tell your Pastor Father, you were having a baby out of wedlock? Well, Daddy didn't scold me or hold it against me, he just said "Okay, let's have a baby!" That was my Dad! And although we ended up thousands of miles away from each other, he was always close by! But my ultimate dream regarding my Father, was when he would be able to marry me to my Boaz. Isn't this every girl's dream?

Then one night, the unthinkable happened. It was around 11:00pm, in February of 1997. I received a call from my Mom in California telling me that my Father had died. Time seemed to have frozen as I tried to formulate in my mind what she just said. Could this be true? He was so young and vibrant! I recall looking around the house to see if everything was in order, as I gathered my thoughts to prepare for this unforeseen journey. Although there were items out of place, it didn't matter. My only focus was getting my son and me to the airport so we could travel to California that night.

For the next week I was in a time warp; empty, no emotions, wondering how I would manage in life without my Dad. Who would be my rock now? Who would help me with my son? Who would cheer me up when I had a rough day? Daddy's smile could pierce any cloudy day and his laugh was contagious. You couldn't help but feel better after speaking to him. In the midst of this tragedy I had to manage preparations for his Memorial and for a huge funeral. Who can think about all of these details when your life was shaken upside down?

The night before the funeral, we had to attend the wake. I dreaded this for this would be the first time I saw my father in months because I lived in Delaware. It was very strange seeing him lying there in the coffin. He didn't look real. The scripture "Yes, we are fully confident, and we would rather be away from these earthly bodies, for then we will be at home with the Lord" (NLT – 2 Corinthians 5:8), was being played out before my eyes. Even though he looked like my father, he wasn't there at all! Truly without his spirit he was lifeless. I said goodbye, but it didn't seem fair that I wasn't able to formally tell him how I felt before he passed away. Nevertheless, I believe he knew that I loved him and would miss him with all of my heart!

The day of the funeral was at finally at hand, the church was overflowing with family and friends. But could I truly maintain my composure? Especially since I was singing my Dad's favorite song – Precious Lord! It was one of the hardest solos I've ever had to sing but God gave me the power to make it through. Once the funeral was over, you could feel the joy in the church. We ended the ceremony with an old favorite hymn "When we all get to Heaven, what a day of rejoicing that will be!" It was definitely a celebration of his life. My Dad, was also a Senior Master Sergeant in the Air Force, so he received a military burial ceremony to honor his service. This included the trumpets playing TAPPS, the color guard and the most memorable event was when the jets flew over our heads.

I was okay through the ceremony, even when they handed the American Flag to my oldest brother. However, at the end they began to roll my Dad away. I screamed "NO" at the top of my lungs as my heart ripped in two. Even though he wasn't physically there, he was still present with me, if that makes any sense. When I saw them rolling him away, I couldn't bear the separation! He was my rock, my friend, my support! He was my hero! No wonder one of our favorite songs, that I used to sing to him, was "Wind beneath my Wings".

A few days after the funeral, it was time for me to come back home. My mom was so concerned about me being in Delaware without any family. But I had to get back to "real life". One thing I decided to do was to create a memory book of my Father. This was very comforting as I dealt with the fact that I would never see him or hear his voice on this side of Heaven again. However, it didn't stop me from crying to sleep for weeks; praying for strength to get through each day! Fortunately, a dear friend of mine shared with me that God loved me more than my father did! In fact, God loved me through my father. The unconditional love and joy my father gave me was birthed from Heaven. It seemed hard to understand at first, but it made sense after a while. It was also hard for me to accept that my Father would not be marrying me as I had dreamed or hoped for. Again my friend revealed to me that my Dad had already married me when he led me to my Savior, Jesus Christ. There was no greater gift of life that my father could have given me than the love of my Lord!

As I prayed daily to my Heavenly Father for strength and comfort for my broken heart, I learned to rely on Him more and more. My relationship with God was growing. One scripture that had a whole new meaning to me was Isaiah 6:1 (NLT) "It was in the year King Uzziah died, that I saw the Lord. He was sitting on a lofty throne, and the train of his robe filled the Temple". You see in the past I looked to my earthly father for everything. He did everything for me! But when he went on to Glory, I now had to look to my Heavenly Father!

What did that mean? It meant that God was now my best friend, my provider, someone who I could talk to and confide in. Every morning, God would give me the beauty of creation and a peace that surpassed all understanding. My Abba Father would give me joy unspeakable and grace that was new every day. Could it be that my relationship with God became alive after the tragic death that occurred in my life.

It's been 17 years since my father went to Glory, even though it feels like yesterday sometimes. And although I miss him, my heart has been restored! I've learned that I've been 'accepted in the beloved.' I was chosen by God before the foundations of the world. God desires me more than I know or understand. I've also realized the unconditional love of God was manifested through my parents and the eyes of my earthly father. I know that my Heavenly Father is my life, my daily portion, my first love! As I seek Him, he reveals the truth of his Word and my purpose to me. Now I can dwell under the shadow of God's wings. I can even mount up on wings like an eagle through every facet of life. God has continually shown me unconditional love and grace. He has truly kept me!

So if you've lost a loved one in your life, I'm here to encourage you that you can still live through the pain of their absence. Your heart will mend as you dwell on the good memories of them. Seek the Lord for strength and peace; not allowing grieve to steal the gift of life from you. Today I can say that God has truly become my Abba Father! And did you know that Abba in Hebrew means "Daddy"! Yes that's right!

I'm still Daddy's Little Girl, just on another dimension!

Gina C. Edwards
Author, Playwriter, Psalmist, Motivational Speaker and Entrepreneur
Bear, DE

"Do not be anxious about anything, but in everything by prayer and supplication with thanksgiving let your requests be made known to God."
Philippians 4:6

I'll Fix It

Sometimes the minutes turned to hours. Sometimes the hours turned into a day. Sometimes the day turned into days. The unpredictability turned into torment. There was no crystal ball that would allow me to see what was going on or to see where he was or wasn't. The truth was evasive yet clear, my decisions were based on emotions and desperation. My emotional state was based on my unwillingness to be transparent, to admit defeat and failure. Failure in my own terms based on my goals and visions.

When people say, "When I get married, divorce is not an option", I shake my head. Who in their right mind gets married to get divorced? The pain that accompanies the journey from the words "I do" to the court approved divorce is not for the weak. You've stood before God and man and vowed 'til death do us part, yet every man's word is not his bond.

My determination to make good on my vows and my pride led me to a place where many would not survive. I survived in the pit of my own darkness by the strength of my children who had no knowledge of my pain. My heart was heavy, my mind a maze; yet my smile was huge, my spirit was strong, and my God was great. But I was broken and humiliated.

From the start it was clear to everyone except for me that this marriage was doomed. But who was anyone to tell me what would or would not work for me. I was independent and I had a dream. My rose-colored glasses and sunny disposition dominated my thoughts. My memory was short. I could do it. I could fix anything and everything that could go wrong. Everything would be ok.

I left the comforts of family and the community I knew and headed off for a military life in unknown parts of the United States. From the moment we were secure in our new surroundings, the turmoil began. There were late nights, early mornings, lies, mysterious calls and unaccounted for spending. Away from all with my pride on the line, I endured. In the midst of the storm, the sun rose up and soothed my troubled mind…my first child, my morning star, my sunshine. It's a girl just for me. She will keep me company and be my companion, my friend, my sanity.

Quickly my happiness returned to turmoil as I clearly remember walking up and down the sidewalk of our apartment complex with my newborn daughter in my arms thinking the worst. This man must be dead. I'll call his first sergeant. There's no way he could just stay out all weekend with no phone call or anything; leaving us alone. Or could he? I'll fix it. Just act like everything is ok and it will be ok. Convinced that being a good wife and good mother could change things, I was determined to fix it.

Nothing changed. But I was changing. Next up, baby number two. Oh to my delight she had my dimples and she was healthy. That was only by God's grace for during my pregnancy with her I was exposed to dangerous elements without my knowledge. I was stunned and humiliated by the revelation during a routine pregnancy exam, which quickly warranted preventative measures. There was no confession, no admission or no acknowledgment. I must be crazy. This can't be. I'll fix it though. God help me.

Let's move back home. Yes! Closer to both of our families and friends, this would work. They would help me fix him. Familiar surroundings, new beginnings, erase the past and start anew. No. It would get worse. Familiar spirits, old stomping grounds, rekindled relationships, déjà vu. And then there were three. But this time it's a boy! We have a chance to raise a man. This would help. He even looks just like me….but sort of like you. No he looks like you but he's my baby….boy.

 Are we fixed yet? Motherhood is great. I flourished in it and accepted all of the responsibilities that came with being a mom. I loved it. No greater joy than these children. They completed me…yet I was empty. The nights were turning into daylight and the daylight into night…again. This is insane. Or maybe it's me. It has to be me. Is there anyone else out there experiencing this? Who can I tell? Where can I run? Where can I hide? Help me…I'm losing me.

Let's move. That will fix it. Wait, I'll move by myself. I can do it. You're coming? Thank you Jesus! We're fixed. Let's go to church. Let's meet new people. Let's start over. We're a family. Wait…why are we in the amusement park? I'm not on the roller coaster; I got off after the last ride. How in the world did I get back here again? You tricked me. You lied. You're killing me. Why is this happening?

So I painted. I painted the most hideous yet beautiful hallway that you have ever seen. I took off from work and painted. I used every paint color imaginable in shapes that looked like they'd been drawn by a two-year old. I painted despite the stares and comments from neighbors and family. It was my hall. No music. No TV. No conversation. Just me, my thoughts and my paint. I found me. But now what? Three children, two dogs, a house on almost an acre of land. Now what?

"Hello? Hello? Are you there? Is your dad home? He's not?! Are you ok? I can't believe this! I'll be home first thing in the morning as soon as the kids wake up. Did you eat? Are you scared? You are so brave. I will call you first thing so keep the phone by you." I think I just died. I did die. Inside. I can't do this anymore. It's not right. I deserve better. How can I escape? What will people think?

"Hey Sonji, give me a call whenever. I've been looking for you."

Mariah Carey on continuous repeat, 'I've loved a lot, hurt a lot. Been burned a lot in my life and times. Spent precious years wrapped up in fear…With no end in sight. Until my saving grace shined on me. Until my saving grace set me free. Giving me peace. Giving me strength when I'd almost lost it all. Catching my every fall. I still exist because you keep me safe. I found my saving grace within you. Yes, I've been bruised. Grew up confused. Been destitute. I've seen life from many sides. Been stigmatized. Been black and white. Felt inferior inside. Until my saving grace shined on me.'

How did he know? How did I get here? Too good to be true. Lord, this is not in the bible anywhere. Is it? Don't you hate divorce? Where did he come from? I made a vow. I've kept my word. Why do I feel guilty? What am I supposed to do? Who am I? Where are these feelings coming from? What will people think? He's crying? You have got to be kidding me! I'm so confused. But I'm not. I'm at peace. I'm listening. I can go. Are you sure God? I'm strong. I can do this. I'm still here. There's peace. There's clarity. This must be God. I'm still here. I'm healed. I'm free. Free to live my life as you have planned for me. Not by my might. Not by my will. Not according to my plan but according to your word. Thank you Jesus! I'm alive and I'm in love…with me. I'm leaving. Today. Right now. Goodness and mercy are following me. My help has come from the hills. I hear you Lord. You fixed me. You fixed it.

Angie Martinez blasting on the radio now, 'If you need it to be, then it can be. It happened for me. It's a new day.'

Sonji Hubbard

Director of Operations, Resh Salon and Spa

Newark, DE

"May the Lord answer you when you are in distress; may the name of the God of Jacob protect you.

2 May he send you help from the sanctuary and grant you support from Zion.
3 May he remember all your sacrifices and accept your burnt offerings.
4 May he give you the desire of your heart and make all your plans succeed.
5 May we shout for joy over your victory and lift up our banners in the name of our God. May the Lord grant all your requests.

6 Now this I know: The Lord gives victory to his anointed. He answers him from his heavenly sanctuary with the victorious power of his right hand.
7 Some trust in chariots and some in horses, but we trust in the name of the Lord our God.
8 They are brought to their knees and fall, but we rise up and stand firm.
9 Lord, give victory to the king! Answer us when we call!"

Psalm 20

My Jehovah Rapha

I always considered myself to be a very active person. I loved going on long walks, and I took every opportunity I could to get exercise. It was nothing for me to run to catch a bus or to walk a mile or more in one day! Pretty good for a 67 year old woman! After retiring from my job I planned on continuing to travel the world and enjoy my life and family so I moved to a new state to be closer to my daughter and grandchild. About a month after I moved I noticed that I was becoming very tired after simple activities like taking a shower or making a cup of tea. I could barely stand up long enough to dress, and going from the kitchen to my bedroom was becoming more and more exhausting. All of my energy seemed to be draining out of my body. As my symptoms progressed, I could hardly even hold a cup to my lips. Instead of my retirement being a joy, I suddenly felt like I had placed a burden on my family.

I saw one doctor after another, but no one could say what was wrong with me. All of my tests came back with great results. On paper, it looked as if I had the health of a thirty year old! After many doctors' visits, hospital visits, and one trip to the emergency department, I was left feeling confused and doubtful. For three months I was bedridden. Prayers were made for me. My pastors prayed, my children prayed, my church members prayed. Everyone I knew was interceding for me! I was reading and meditating on God's Word. I know that healing is the children's bread. I know that by His stripes we were healed. I knew these things, but I was waiting to see it manifest in my life.

One day, as my son and I were discussing healing in the Bible, he mentioned the most profound thing. He said that the woman with the issue of blood TOOK her healing from Jesus. He said Jesus stopped so that she could reach down and touch his garment. At that moment a light came to me.

I said that I too can TAKE my healing from Jesus. From that day on I have been confessing that "Just from Jesus simply taking life and rest and joy and peace and HEALING!"

And from that day my body began to heal. I am no longer suffering waves of exhaustion. I am up and about, going for walks, helping around the house, and enjoying my life again. In fact, I'll be going on an island vacation in the next few weeks!

God, the Great Physician, healed my body without **any** medication, and to Him be the glory!

Joyce Schultz
Elementary School Teacher (Retired), Author
Slidell, LA

"At that time Jesus answered and said, I thank thee, O Father, Lord of heaven and earth, because thou hast hid these things from the wise and prudent and hast revealed them unto babes. 26 Even so, Father: for so it seemed good in thy sight. 27 All things are delivered unto me of my Father: and no man knoweth the Son, but the Father; neither knoweth any man the Father, save the Son, and he to whomsoever the Son will reveal him. 28 Come unto me, all ye that labour and are heavy laden, and I will give you rest. 29 Take my yoke upon you, , and learn of me; for I am meek and lowly in heart: and ye shall find rest unto your souls 30 For my yoke is easy and my burden is light."

Matthew 11:25-30

Finding the God in Me

My life has been a journey of self-discovery, a discovery of the precious, intelligent, sweet and gentle soul God created me to be from the moment of conception. This is my story, my testimony of how I overcame the darkest of times in my life and let the light of God shine through me.

For some people, there is one (1) major event that changes their lives in such a way where they can never return to the person they once were. For me, I have had several major events that have made me the person I am today. I am a survivor of: cancer, abuse (mental, emotional, sexual and physical), infertility and depression. As I share my testimony with all of you, as I air my dirty laundry in hopes of letting you know that you are not alone in your pain, I could share my experience with any of the above listed traumas, but I will choose one, the one I believe caused me the greatest pain and helped me to experience my greatest victory.

I grew up an only child of very well-off parents; my father was a high school administrator and the first African American principal in a nearby town. My mother was a stunningly beautiful woman, the kind of beautiful that caused people to stop and stare and my father loved that about her. There was only one problem with this young couple who seem to have it all, they were barren. After being married for 17 years they were unable to have a child. This left my mother devastated as she desperately wanted a child. So they decided to adopt a child and during their search, they found a little baby girl, born on my father's birthday, needless to say he was sold. I was adopted at the age of three weeks old and now this family was "seemingly" perfect.

Once I was adopted I quickly became a "daddy's girl". My father immediately loved me and soon I became the center of his world. My mother grew increasingly jealous and took her childish feelings out on a vulnerable child who only wanted to be loved. My relationship with my adopted mother was a painful one and one that placed deep wounds in my soul and my psyche.

It wasn't until years later that I discovered my mother suffered from chronic depression and bi-polar disorder. She treated both illnesses with alcohol and during the most formative years of my life she was a violent alcoholic. My parents were socialites and were always attending lavish parties and I can remember them coming home from these parties and my mother being drunk and stumbling in the house, unable to walk or function. I can also remember hearing her vomit the next morning; I would take a pillow and put it over my head to drown out the noise. But what I remember the most is the horrible things she would say to me when she was drunk, there was one statement in particular that changed the nature of our relationship forever. One day, while floating in her swimming chair in our beautiful in-ground pool, she looked at me and said these words "sometimes I think the worst mistake we ever made was getting you". As an 11 year old child, it took me years to recover from those words. From that point on, even as a child, I knew I did not have a mother, not one who would love me unconditionally. I knew from that point on that there was a part of my mother that regretted my existence and that I was not completely welcome in my own "home". The place where I was supposed to be the safest is the place where I received my deepest wounds and my darkest pain. Nothing made this more obvious than the day I was physically attacked by my mother.

Even as an eleven year old child, I knew the pain I was carrying was real, the daily insults that were hurled at me, the way she looked at me, the lack of affection she showed me, I knew I didn't belong in that house and one day I decided to do something about it. I wanted escape from her drinking, and from the unbearable pain I was feeling so one day I decided to run away. I never wanted to return to that house, I never wanted to see my mother's face again, so I decided to take my friend's bus home from school with her and figure things out from there. This was a pretty well laid out plan for a sixth grader, one that was foolproof. I didn't know what I would do from day to day, but I knew returning to my place of pain simply was not an option. As it turns out, my plan was not as foolproof as I thought. While I was at my friend's house, I heard the doorbell ring and the voice was familiar, it was the voice of my father. He had deep concern in his voice and he told my friend's aunt that I had run away and he was there to take me "home". I remember feeling my heart drop to my knees, my plan had failed and I was headed back to the house of pain.

As I rode home with my father I can remember him sounding disappointed and relieved all at the same time. I knew I was in trouble, but nothing could have prepared me for what was going to take place when I got home. As my father and I walked into the door, I can remember the look of anger on my mother's face, I almost stopped breathing. I remember being asked to sit down in our living room, my parents asked me why I ran away and I pointed to my mother and said "because of her". The next thing I remember is feeling her fist pounding on my head and my face. The assault started in our living room and ended in the kitchen, five minutes which seemed like an eternity of her punching me and screaming at me, I remember saying "I'm sorry" over and over again, but sadly my apologies fell on deaf ears. The one thing that was as equally painful as the beating I took that night was the way my father stood by, and even encouraged my mother. He said I deserved what I got and that I should have been ashamed for trying to leave such a "loving" family. Obviously he was in denial and I realized at that point I had no one, no one in this world to protect me.

After the assault, I remember having a horrible headache, as if I had been in a street fight with a grown woman, well, actually I had. I went into the bathroom, looked in the mirror and was in sheer horror of what I saw. My face was swollen and battered, my lips were busted and I could barely see straight. I tried my best to sleep that night, but I couldn't help but think she was coming to hurt me again and I was glad to see the sun come up, which meant I had made it through the night without being attacked again.

The next day I went to school and just before I left my mother spoke these words "unless you want it to happen again, you better not tell anyone what happened". From that day I learned to lie about what I was feeling and I have spent at least two decades unlearning; the first is: what I think and how I feel do not matter; the second is: it is okay for people who say they love me to hurt me and three: I am not worthy of being loved.

Those three lies kept me in bondage for many, many years. I ended up in toxic relationships, I lost my voice, and simply began to "go with the flow" scared that if I made waves I would be attacked again or I wouldn't have any friends. Even the men who did truly and honestly care for me did not stand a chance because I had the belief I did not deserve love, so I sabotaged even the good relationships I had.

I remember going through life thinking I had done something terribly wrong for my birth mother to have given me away and for me to get another mother who hated me, I simply did not deserve love. I sought comfort in food and at one point, this 5'2 woman, reached 225 pounds. I also began drinking just as my mother did and ended up in toxic relationships with men who only wanted my body and treated me poorly. I tried drugs and even decided to get married; thinking marriage would "heal" me and fill all the empty spaces in my life. Sadly my marriage ended after six years. When I married I was still having a difficult time dealing with the fact that my childhood was taken from me so viciously and methodically. I was still very angry and heartbroken for the little girl inside of me who never had a chance to experience a full, happy, safe childhood.

Often I hear people tell of a "come to Jesus" moment in their lives, where anything that was painful or any damaged place within them was miraculously healed the day they gave their lives to God. I have always envied those people. My healing process had been anything but "instantaneous". My healing process has been a combination of a belief that I could be healed, dedication to the painful process of healing and making a conscious decision to replace self-hatred with the love of God and a healthy dose of the love of self.

I have sought healing almost all my life in one way or another, but it was a few years after my divorce that I really stopped playing the role of the victim, although I certainly was a "victim" in many ways as a child. The first step to healing, after accepting God's love for us, is to move from being a victim to learning how to process the pain we have encountered. Playing the role of the victim, repeating the horrible things that were done to us and continuing to feel sorry for what has happened to us, keeps us trapped in "victim" mode. Now, there is a time in the healing process when you certainly do need to acknowledge and grieve what has happened to us, but at some point, you must receive God's love for you, the love you've been searching and seeking for all your life, and begin to start living the full, abundant life God has called us to live.

When you receive God's love, you let down the walls of your heart and you let God in. Many of us who have been hurt by those closest to us have a hard time even letting God into our hearts. But you must remember that God is not man, God is not who hurt you, God is a healer and is eager to heal the broken places in you, but you MUST make a decision to trust God and trust that the love of God can make you whole again. You must believe that God can make the rest of your life, the best of your life. You must begin to see yourself as God sees you and God sees you as someone worthy of being loved. Once you get that belief deep in your soul, you will begin to see those who have hurt you so terribly in a different light.

After receiving God's love for me and beginning an intimate relationship with our great God, I realized that what happened to me was not my fault and that I was indeed worthy of receiving love. I realized that my mother was sick and that somewhere in her life; she had not been introduced to God's love or rejected it altogether. I realized that every person walking this Earth is deserving of love, God's love and healthy relationships that reflect God's love.

So no matter where you are today, no matter how deep your pain is, how broken your heart may be or how low you feel; I want you to know there is hope for you, genuine hope. God's love is abundant and is not picky. God doesn't care what you look like, how much money you make or how many times people have hurt you. God's love is looking for you and waiting for you to give up all of yourself, not just the parts you like, but even the messy, ugly parts of yourself; give it all to God. It starts with a belief, you MUST believe that God wants an abundant life for you, and then the journey to wholeness will begin. Do you believe? I hope so...

Charmagne R. Quarles, M.Ed.
Philadelphia, PA

"But he said to me, "My grace is sufficient for you, for my power is made perfect in weakness." Therefore I will boast all the more gladly of my weaknesses, so that the power of Christ may rest upon me." 2 Corinthians 12:9

I'm More Than My Failures

My story starts when I was in elementary school, but I'll come back to that later. Fast forward to me as a 19 year old girl used to being above average in every aspect of her life. Education, social circles, talents, etc., all came easy to me…until now! My second year of college a few things happened. First, I got a part time job and excelled, becoming one of the top sales associates. This was an issue because now I only wanted to work and make more and more money. "For the love of money is a root of all kinds of evil. Some people, eager for money, have wandered from the faith and pierced themselves with many griefs." (1 Timothy 6:10) Second, classwork didn't come so easy anymore and I actually had to study! This was going to be a challenge considering I wanted to work more and more hours. Christmas break came, and so did my report card. I'd been placed on academic probation and could not return the following semester. I felt ashamed, like a failure. How could the girl voted Most Likely to Succeed flunk out of college? My parents were not pleased. I come from a family of educators and my parents were very focused on my education and academic prowess. It would be another 10 years before I finished my bachelor's degree.

At the ripe old age of 23, I got married. I'd always wanted to be married, have someone to come home to everyday, to cook for, have a constant friend to talk to, etc. He was a great person who I could talk to about anything and we enjoyed hanging out together. There was one problem…neither of us really knew how to be a husband or wife. I was impatient and didn't allow time for us to grow. My mentality was that I did not have time to waste on something that's not working and to get rid of 'things' quickly if they weren't making me happy. I didn't use the great communication we had to try to work through the issues and build a stronger foundation. I didn't use the scriptures to strengthen me for the spiritual warfare that ensues when two come together. "Love is patient, love is kind…It always protects, always trusts, always hopes, always perseveres." (1 Corinthians 13: 4-7) In the end, I cheated on my husband, and even though he was willing to continue to work on the marriage, I decided I wanted out so we got a divorce. Add another shameful failure to add to my list.

Still in my 20s, I got into a relationship with a new man. We had a great time together and often were the center of our social circle. We traveled, experienced new adventures together, laughed a lot and had a common affinity for the love of sports. Sounded like a great combination, so we decided to get married. I'm still that domestic personality you met when I was 23 so being someone's wife seems like a great idea. I mean, we seem to get along well, why not? We are married for a couple of years when we decide to have a baby. Our beautiful little girl is born and I start back attending church on a regular basis, but unfortunately we only stay married another few years. Remember when I said 'why not' get married? I should've been asking myself 'why' instead. While I was having fun, my need to be with someone had me blatantly ignoring all of the warning signals that told me without a shadow of a doubt I should not be in this relationship, let alone be married. When I got back into church, God revealed so many things to me. "Therefore judge nothing before the appointed time; wait until the Lord comes. He will bring to light what is hidden in darkness and will expose the motives of the heart. At that time each will receive their praise from God." (1 Corinthians 4:5) Now there's another life affected by my decisions which I don't seem to be making very well up until this point.

In my 30s, I've now achieved my Master's degree (my mother is very proud), and I've done a lot of soul searching. I'm starting to realize who I am as a woman, how valuable I am as a person, and that I need to look out for myself before all else. This means that I had to lose some people in my life, let go of the shame and regret, start thinking about my needs and my daughter's needs. I began attending church on a regular basis and participating in the music ministry, life began to calm down and I had some really good friends supporting me through the latest chapter in my life. One of those friends, I started connecting to on an intellectual and emotional level. As we talked more and more, our connection grew and we started dating. We were both shocked and amazed at how well we'd connected, but also that we were dating our friend. "God has a great sense of humor", I'd think to myself. But God always has a plan even when we can't see it or understand it. "For I know the plans I have for you," declares the Lord, "plans to prosper you and not to harm you, plans to give you hope and a future." (Jeremiah 29:11) The person we'd been asking God for, the one he'd planned for this moment in time was right there all the time. We couldn't see it behind the 'velvet curtains'. You've seen velvet curtains. They are thick so no light can pass through and you can't see through them. They are heavy and hard to move. Our 'velvet curtains' were relationships with the wrong people, standards for who we wanted versus what we needed, childhood hang ups, etc. We talked about marriage but only as a 'what if' or 'what would it be like'. See this guy has been married before and wants to get it right. And I'm thinking there is no way I should get married again! This would be number 3, what would people say? They said a lot by the way, good and bad. I was scared; if I'm being honest, but little did I know this guy was about to overcome his hang ups and ask me to marry him. I'm sure you saw that coming given what I've disclosed about my history, but understand that I thought I was through with the whole wife thing. However, I'm not through, and number 3 is now my husband.

Today I am in my 40s and want to share with you what I've learned from these experiences. Here's where I take you back to my elementary school days. Those formative years that build the foundation for what we'll become. It was during those years that I was raised and molded into a perfectionist with low self-esteem. Under the guise of striving for excellence, a bar was set for me that said average is not good enough, even if it was your best. An example would be making all A's with one A-, and being asked why you got the minus. Being raised like this did a few things. One, it cultivated a personality trait that causes me to stress when I can't be flawless. Performance reviews, grade reports, being a wife and mother, being a singer…all give me anxiety because I want to be flawless at it. Two, it strained the relationship I had with my mother because I never felt like I could please her. Another foundation that was laid during my early years was self-esteem…or the lack thereof. While I was very popular, being dark skinned and skinny wasn't exactly the 'in' thing and I laugh as I thank God I've 'blossomed' as I've aged. With all of these 'foundations' to build my life on, I've journeyed through my years consistently letting them plague my decisions and thoughts of myself. "If I can't be perfect then I don't want to finish it." This is how I flunked out of college. "I must keep getting promotions to be seen as successful." This is how I ended up in jobs I didn't want. However, the biggest impact has been on my self-esteem. I believe it to be the reason I spent my life searching for love and acceptance in the places they were not. I accepted less than I deserved because I'd failed in the past or because I wasn't sure I was worthy of more. Did you keep count all of my failures? I used to, but now I know God doesn't. Where I saw failure, each time God saw an opportunity to position me for more. So I learned that I am not perfect. I will make mistakes. I must learn from those situations but more importantly, know that does not have to be the end of my story. From my failed marriages I learned patience. Patience with other people and patience in waiting on God. From flunking out of school, I learned discipline. Discipline in accomplishing what I need to get done and not letting distractions get in the way of me achieving my goals. What I've learned through all of it is resilience and faith. It's not the failure that has the most impact, it's how I handle it, how I bounce back, how I learn and move forward and have faith that God is. Because God is "I can do all this through him who gives me strength." (Philippians 4:13) Because God is…He will prosper me in those things He's ordained, and remove those things that are not. I just have to speak it, claim it, and believe it.

While I am still a work in progress, what I know for sure is God had and still has His hands on me. My life of shame, regret, and failure God turned into my testimony. The testimony I share with you today that says you're more than a conqueror, you are not what others think of you and more than what you think of yourself, you are worthy of the love God meant for you. You are 'fearfully and

wonderfully made' (Psalm 139:14). You are God's child.

Kellye R Hubbard
Recording Artist
Washington, DC

"There Hath no temptation taken you but such as is common to man: but God is faithful, who will not suffer you to be tempted above that ye are able; but will with the temptation also make a way to escape, that ye may be able to bear it." 1 Corinthians 10:13

The Wait

As I look back over my life it comes to mind that I have so much to be thankful for. Sometimes the adverse issues, circumstances and situations that I have faced try to overwhelm the joyous overcomes that God has given me.

When my husband transitioned from life on this earth December 2, 2005 I wasn't thinking about my future in terms of ever getting married again. It felt like a part of me had died. I had no clue how the journey into widowhood would change my life.

I have decided to share my testimony of living a life of celibacy until God sends me a mate. As I write this it has been at least 11 years since I have had sexual intimacy with a man. I have fully considered the fact that I may never have the privilege of being a wife again, but one thing I do know is "My maker is my husband". Rickey was diagnosed with prostate cancer in early 2003 after he had lost a lot of weight. I didn't know much about prostate cancer so I wasn't aware of how devastating it could be. The cancer had metastasized spreading to his liver, spine and brain eventually causing paralysis from his waist down.

We come to a place in our lives where life decisions have to be made. Of course being faithful to my wedding vows wasn't difficult, I made them before God and I meant every word. So even though I was approached by men (some claiming to be saved) who suggested that I take care of my neglected physical needs; I kept my vows.

We can hold on to our convictions when there is a tangible person there to remind us that we have a promise to keep. After Rickey's death I was so consumed with trying to breathe again being made love to was the least of my concerns. Actually the first five years I just focused on trying to keep my finances afloat. I was left without enough insurance and a very large house note. I discovered that men somehow think you are a "sugga momma" if you are a widow; some of them 20 or more years younger were making contact for a date. I am now grateful for all of the attempts they made and the flattering words about how beautiful they think I am. One thing I have learned is that as soon as you take a stand for righteousness their true colors are revealed. One such person told me even if I didn't have sex with him, he could say I did and somebody would believe him. My response: "I will make sure that I attend your funeral so that I can explain your sudden death after you lied on God's daughter." I could speak this with conviction because I have submitted myself to God to be holy and acceptable unto him and he has kept me chaste and preserved for my mate.

I would be remiss if I leave out the times that the temptation was presented and I truly desired to be with that certain man. That's when the true test of the wait revealed itself. He was tall, dark, handsome and oh yes, he looked good, smelled good and had the goods to take care of me. This is when I had to find scripture to apply to my situation just as I did during my personal battle with cancer. My favorite scripture to confess out loud daily: 1 Corinthians 6:16-20 The Message Bible (MSG) There's more to sex than mere skin on skin. Sex is as much spiritual mystery as physical fact. As written in Scripture, "The two become one." Since we want to become spiritually one with the Master, we must not pursue the kind of sex that avoids commitment and intimacy, leaving us lonely than ever— the kind of sex that can never "become one." There is a sense in which sexual sins are different from all others. In sexual sin we violate the sacredness of our own bodies, these bodies that were made for God-given and God-modeled love, for "becoming one" with another. Or didn't you realize that your body is a sacred place, the place of the Holy Spirit? Don't you see that you can't live however you please, squandering what God paid such a high price for? The physical part of you is not some piece of property belonging to the spiritual part of you. God owns the whole work. So let people see God in and through your body.

So now I die daily to my personal need for companionship, intimacy or even a passionate kiss. It has not been easy, but it is doable. I share this testimony so that not only a widow in waiting, but all ladies in waiting will make a choice to serve God with a pure heart. There is nothing between the sheets worth giving up your spiritual oneness with God.

And when that special someone comes along you will recognize him because you have had your ear tuned in to the heartbeat of God. I am an older woman and many young ladies that I have counseled feel that I couldn't possibly know their struggle; I beg to differ. Having known the pleasure of enjoying love making within the covenant of marriage for twenty nine and a half years then to withdraw cold turkey is no picnic. It is in the senior years of a mature woman that she realizes how this thing works and how phenomenal this thing is that God created and equipped us to enjoy. The decision to remain celibate has been one I am so glad I made. Though sometimes lonely and feeling abandoned, holding onto God's promise that he would never leave me or forsake me has proven to be so true in my real life issues and situations. I am grateful to God that neither my desires nor my financial status motivated me to walk outside of his will for my life. I can cheerfully say my financial needs have been met with the amazing doors that God has opened for me in ministry and in my retirement.

Through this journey I have learned some things about me. First of all, I had to release my husband and move forward. It was very difficult to accept that I am no longer a married woman. Secondly, I had to allow God to be my husband; submitting to him and allowing him to have leadership in every area of my life. We often think we have surrendered all and then discover that there's that one other thing which remains hidden in the clutches of our control.

Thirdly, I now know that when my mate arrives he will be a complete man of God, no insecurities or doubts about what he hears from God. I haven't been waiting for God to send my mate; God has been waiting for me to be ready to receive him. I must be a vessel with no leaky places, properly prepared to be a help meet that brings God glory. I have learned it is worth the wait to be in God's perfect will. I am single, but nothing is missing because I am an individual fearfully and wonderfully made by God. I am uniquely made whole because of the sacrifice he made; giving his life so that I could be called his very own lacking nothing.

Ladies of all ages I want to encourage you to stop looking for love in all the wrong places. Stop seeking a man to satisfy your longings thus giving birth to babies out of your pain. With all of the baby mama - baby daddy drama, even in the church it is time to choose a better way. The author and the finisher is the only one who can fill the void. Please receive his love today. I did and I am happy and content during 'The Wait'.

Psalm 27:14 Wait on the LORD: be of good courage, and he shall strengthen thine heart: wait, I say, on the LORD.

Psalm 130:5 I wait for the LORD, my soul doth wait, and in his word do I hope.

1 Corinthians 6:18 (KJV) Flee fornication. Every sin that a man doeth is without the body; but he that committeth fornication sinneth against his own body.

1 Thessalonians 4:3-5 King James Version (KJV) For this is the will of God, even your sanctification, that ye should abstain from fornication: That every one of you should know how to possess his vessel in sanctification and honour; Not in the lust of concupiscence, even as the Gentiles which know not God:

Faye Mosby

Recording Artist, Author

Little Rock, AR

"Come near to God and he will come near to you "
James 4:8

"All things work for the good, for those who love God and are called according to his purpose."
Romans 8:28

DESTINY CHILD

This testimony is about issues experienced and speaks to teen pregnancy, abortion, oppression from abuse, failure in marriage resulting in divorce, single parenting, finances and rape. This just covers a few. You may be thinking, you mean there is more. I only hope that through this real life story and transparency, you will be encouraged to know that no matter the kind of hand life has dealt you, or if you made bad decisions, there is always hope as long as you have life and keep the FAITH in God.

On Friday, November 22, 1946 there were torrential downpours of rain when a teenage girl 14 yrs. old was rushed to the hospital by her father to give birth to a baby girl at about 9:30 P.M. This poor girl had no idea what was happening to her except that she was about to become a mother. As you know, in that era, parents didn't talk to girls about the birds and the bees. There was no family planning agency, (DAPI) Delaware Adolescent Program, Inc. for pregnant teens or birth control pills, etc. To compound her problem, she had an angry bitter mother at home who chose not to accompany her to the hospital for the delivery of the first grandchild.

During that time it was most embarrassing and unacceptable to be pregnant and not be married. Unlike today's time, when it is almost seemingly popular to be a teenage unwed mother. Some would say it's the norm. The government and school systems cooperate to support teenage pregnancy. Am I against the help? No, but I know we should put more emphasis for a need to help show them a better way to start their life and evaluate their values.

This young girl, while pregnant was sent away to live with family in Georgia. Because her visit with family didn't work out, she was returned to her hometown up north, to live with a mother who had no compassion for her and to face the shame that came with the territory. I can't imagine the fear this young girl must have felt. The father was a teen of 16 yrs. old and had no idea what he had done or the kind of responsibility he or she was facing in life. At age 16 she was given consent to get married to an older guy and gave birth to 12 more children. The father married another and fathered 9 kids. Both parents of the baby girl have since passed away. The mother passed away on July 27, 2006 and the father passed away on August 16, 2012.

This story reminds me somewhat of Mary the mother of Jesus who found herself with child and was embarrassed about her pregnancy until she heard directly from God. I am so glad that this young girl's parents somehow heard the voice of God and did not force this teenage mom to abort the pregnancy. That would have aborted the PLAN of GOD. We know today, abortion has become a legal weapon to take a life. When afforded the opportunity, I always encourage women not to abort a life. God should be the only giver and taker of life. I tell them you may be murdering the next president, doctor, teacher, preacher and whomever God is sending to do His Will. It could be the very one who will BLESS your life.

As history continues to be written and sometimes repeats itself. Life for the baby girl born on Nov. 22 mirrored a lot of what her mother had gone through at home, being parented by a bitter wife, mother, and extreme dysfunction and an alcoholic. This is what probably propelled her mother to look for love in the wrong direction. After finishing high school, at the young age of 18 she married a young Christian boy, age 19 and both his parents were Pastors. Naturally, she thought she was on the right track. Isn't that what we were taught in that era? Finish school and marry a good Christian man or a good man. She was hardly prepared for marriage but it seemed like a safe escape to get away from this dysfunction called home. Although she was privileged with many material things, there was a lot of anger and pain inflicted on her by the grandmother. There was not much care and compassion of a mother's love. On the other hand, the grandfather was the light of her life and was always there for her. I'm sure none of this sounds unfamiliar to you. But I hope if you are a mother reading this, that it will be a mirror for you to look at and find out how important your role is as a mother. If you are a father and reading this, I hope the same.

To fast forward at the age of 20, she gave birth to her firstborn a boy. Shortly after the birth of her first born, here comes the grand plan and scheme of the enemy. Her husband abruptly without rhyme or reason decided to move to NYC almost immediately. She left her 9 month old son with her mother-in-law to move to NYC and lived there for about 12 years. Living in NYC was exciting and an interesting experience. However, she didn't use a GPS to get there. Living in NYC took her life somewhere she would never want to go again. For a short while life was good. Jobs were easy to get. A high school education was rated pretty high at that time. She met a lot of important and famous people. But had forgot about the most famous one, (God) in her life. But Life happened. She was still afraid and not understanding how to end this abusive marriage. She had a second child, a baby girl. This pregnancy happened while separated from this marriage. The marriage was very violent and abusive. Prior to the birth of her baby girl, she had a miscarriage and later a forced abortion. That's another pain that seems to linger.

In 1976 she was raped and seriously injured by a stranger who was found guilty and convicted of raping several women in the NYC area. This was during the time that the AIDS epidemic was on the rise. Knowing this, can you imagine the fear she must have felt as a result of the rape. Yes, I guess that could have happened anywhere, not just NYC. But when it happens to you, believe me something changes inside of you forever. You are never the same.

Finally, she is AWAKENED after a STORMY life experience of allowing herself to be led in the wrong direction. She made immature and bad decisions that were not God directed. She was abused beaten, abandoned and left for another women and no family in NYC to turn to. She decided to listen to the voice of God and return to her place of DESTINY, home.

She single parented for 10 years with no financial support from her two children's father. However, her grandparents would lend financial help as would the mother-in-law and father-in-law when needed. There were still many tough times to deal with trying to get to her DESTINY, the PLAN God had for her. She lived with (in-laws) family for a short period until she was able to secure a job and a place of her own. This was a new experience being on her own to raise her children alone. She escaped the abusive marriage and divorced. She still experienced pain and flashbacks of the abuse including the rape. It was a hard challenge to make the break and she still had to extend a father's rights to visitation by a court order. There is more gloom and doom to this story, but not enough time to tell. More of life happened that caused much devastation. Such as; having to relocate too many times because of financial circumstances and sometimes strange things that were unexplainable at the time. This would of course affect the school the children would attend. Those bumpy trials certainly had an effect on her mental stability and the kids. The abuse of the now ex-husband didn't stop in NYC. He later arrived to their new home in a different state to continue to inflict pain on the mother and the children. But thanks, be to God, somebody PRAYED and it all ceased.

A NEW BEGINNING … in July of 1985 something happened and everything changed for this baby girl born on Nov 22, 1946. She met her BOAZ. The man God had CHOSEN for her. Although this was the PLAN of God, they met much opposition. But isn't that always the case with the ENEMY. They TRUSTED and BELIEVED God through all the opposition and in 1988 she married her

BOAZ. They both came with baggage and pain from their previous relationships. But because of God's PLAN they have been together for 30 years and married for twenty-seven years. The reason for the three year gap is because of the previous abusive relationship, she had much fear to marry again. But God's PLAN for them prevailed. There have been many challenges in this marriage and still are from time to time. But this marriage has been a diamond in the rough and has withstood the ever burning fire that continues to destroy marriages today.

I am the baby that was born on Nov. 22, 1946 and the author of this testimony.

I sometimes recall the stories my mother and father shared with me about what they remembered and learned about their experience of becoming teenage parents. That would be another book. I was raised by my maternal grandparents who both have passed away. Although my grandmother was abusive, I believe she loved me in her own dysfunctional way. I learned that hurt people hurt people. My grandfather was a hardworking, meek and humble man. He loved all of his children and family and was well liked in his community.

Life threw me a lot of bad punches, but no matter the devils plan, it didn't work. I'm still here. No matter the circumstance, it is how you respond to the situation that you are faced with. As you probably could tell I had no real help or counsel about getting married or about parenting. I just bumped into wall after wall trying to figure life out and found myself married to a confused angry boy who had lost his way. Today my children's father and I are very civil to one another and sometimes attend the same social gatherings. Above all we have FORGIVEN each other for all the pain we shared. How are our two children? They have suffered much as a result of that bad marriage. But we talk a lot and are very close. They are age 48 and 45. I am proud to say they are both SAVED and practicing Christians. Of course, they still have life issues to deal with, but I have through the knowledge of God taught WISDOM nuggets of how to respond to have a successful end. The Bible says young women listen the older women and young men listen to the older men. They are experienced. (Titus 2:4-7)

If you are single I advise that you get to know who you are and stay close to God and allow him to lead you to your mate. If you want to have a successful marriage, be honest and communicate with one another and above all keep God first in everything you do.

The family unit is important and critical in providing a sound firm foundation for your children. About parenting, your children are watching the movie, so be mindful of how you live your life.

Today I and my Boaz are ordained ministers. He is an ordained Elder/Pastor and I have been ordained as a Reverend and to the Office of the Evangelist. I say to folks all the time ……. "You don't know my story, you just see GOD's GLORY"

The lesson I have learned is, it was never about me, but God only using my mess to bless someone else. God's Plan will PREVAIL. You just need the right (GPS) GOD's PLAN SAVES. If you don't use it, you will lose it. This is just an excerpt to my story.

Prayerfully submitted,

Destiny Child

Come near to God and he will come near to you (James 4:8)

All things work for the good, for those who love God and are called according to his purpose.

(Romans 8:28)

Rev. Lorraine Dryden
New Castle, DE

"The Lord is close to the broken hearted and saves those who are crushed in spirit."

Psalm 34:18

A New Heart

I got married at the age of 23. I had a fairy tale wedding; it was absolutely beautiful! I thought I would be married forever, but within the first few months of marriage it began to go "south" I thought it would change, and he would change but he never did. Within two months of being married I became pregnant. I believed the pregnancy would change and mature my then husband. But instead it just got worst. I discovered that although he wanted to be married, he was not ready to give up the single, partying life and I on the other hand, was ready to be a wife.

Both of us were pastor's kids, we grew up in the church but neither of us was serving the Lord! While we were dating, we both partied . . . a lot! Why would I think he would change by himself, without the Lord; it never happened. Not too long after our son was born we separated. As a matter of fact we separated a couple of times. Before our second year of marriage, I filed for divorce. It was very difficult for me because I grew in a Christian home where divorce was not an option. I never discussed it with my family. I didn't tell them that I filed for divorce; I did not want them to talk me out of it. All I knew is that I could not live my life in turmoil. I cut myself of from my family and I decided that I would go through it myself.

Once the divorce was final, I told my family. I was so hurt and lost and faced with the reality that now I am a single mother. Something I never thought I would be. My family embraced me. And my father tried to help me heal. I remember my mother telling me that she wished I would have told them so they could have been there to support me. I locked them out because they had a perfect example of a good marriage, and my marriage failed! I felt as if I committed the "unthinkable" sin. But I found out I did not.

In the efforts to hide my hurt I began to party again with one of my friends. I was a mother during the day, took care of my son and partied in the night. I began to hang out with "new" friends who never went to church and were not thinking about going. My life was spiraling out of control. I had no joy or peace and I felt so condemned. I was also struggling to be a good mother; therefore, I overcompensated and gave my son whatever he wanted.

One day I was coming back from out of town with my nephew and son when we got into an accident that if God did not step in we would have been dead. I remember screaming "Jesus" when the accident took place and immediately He came to our rescue. I don't remember much after calling Jesus; I just remember the police and ambulance being there and them expecting us to be dead. I was so grateful that I began going back to church. I rededicated my life back to God and began serving Him. One Sunday evening I was in service and the pastor began to minister on Ezekiel 36. Verse 26 states "A new heart also will I give you, and a new spirit will I put within you: and I will take away the stony heart out of your flesh, and I will give you a heart of flesh." KJV That night I went home and prayed that scripture. I told God that I needed a new heart because I was so hurt that I could not function any longer with the hurt heart. He heard me and gave me a new heart and a new spirit that night! I felt the pain, hurt and condemnation removed. I felt free and alive again! God did a miracle in me!! Not too long after that I went to the doctor for a check-up. I have had a heart murmur for years and on that visit, the doctor told me that my heart murmur was no longer there... God still does miracles! I was so excited because God did surgery on me; I was no longer the same.

This year I will be married 27 years to my friend, lover, and my Man of God who loves me to life. I am so grateful to

God for what He has done for me. How He has blessed and moved in my life words cannot explain! There is life after divorce and with God there is no condemnation ... you can live again. If you are hurting from divorce and feel as if all is lost; know that it is not! God can do surgery on you and give you a new heart ... just ask him!

Pastor Esther Graham
Dover, DE

"So the last will be first, and the first will be last."
Matthew 20:16

The Least Likely But, Through God I Did.

I am the oldest in my family. If you know anything about birth order, the oldest is usually the most conservative, the leader, the stick close to home and usually not the radical, maverick of the family. You know the "miss goody two shoes." My two younger sisters are the vocal, headstrong and strong-willed members of my family. When you are naturally easy going and don't make waves you don't think bad things are going to happen to you. Some situations are not bad they are just life. Over the years, I have had to learn that hard lesson. The phrase, "why me, what did I do to deserve this," resonated repeatedly in my heart and mind. God in all of His wisdom decided that in spite of my temperament He must add a tougher more resilient component to my personality, will and fortitude. A soldier can't always avoid conflict but, be ready to go boldly into battle. He did it through heartache, disappointment and love. First, God made me fall in love with Him so much that I was willing to follow Him anywhere. He also made me trust Him even though I made mistakes, stumbled and made many bad choices. He also taught me how to hear Him in the best place, on the back side of the mountain, alone. He worked it all out for my good.

I was the typical kid with glasses, chubby, bad feet, and sinus trouble but, with an extrovert personality and musical gift straight from God that helped soften much heartache. In 1986, I married the guy that all of the single girls at my church wanted. How do I know? He was tall, a Texan, no kids, a soldier, a chef, loved God and served in church faithfully. He was an usher and after he lead the people around for offering, he came back with small pieces of paper with other women's phone numbers on them while we were dating and had publicly announced our engagement. He embarrassed many young woman each week, with me on the other line telling them that he wasn't interested. Goodbye and God bless. We were married but, the life we planned ended by the one woman he couldn't say no to, his mother. End of story. I was devastated to say the least but, returned home to a supportive family that did everything in their power to help erase his memory. I was single, no children and he refused to help pay bills that we made together. What do you do next? I cried buckets of tears, prayed fervently, worked long hours and rebuilt my life. I worked in the day, enrolled in school as well as taught night classes after work and then cleaned buildings at night school classes. I sang, travelled and continued to love God in spite of my heartache.

One thing that I have learned when you fall in love to God, He will show Himself strong in your life and miracles will manifest. My divorce was free other than the filing fee. God opened a door for me to receive three post graduate degrees free. I began writing poetry, music, recording music and building a new life based on the purpose that God designed for me.

I not only experienced the divorce from a husband. I had to divorce my home church. My season there had come to an end and with my pastor's blessing, I began to support and help church plants to grow. I received a prophecy that I would be sent out and possibly to the nations. I was raised in a very conservative denomination but, realized that my allegiance had to be to God and Him, alone. Leaving one denomination and because of my gift, ministering in many different church settings has given me an experience with God and ministry unparalleled. I was released from a church but, I was never released from God. God is who I worship and Him alone. God allowed me to work, learn, teach and train several music ministers, department ministry leaders and assist many pastors to grow and mature God's people. I initially left my home church, scared, scarred and insecure. Now my fear is faith, scars are not a secret and the insecurities are eliminated. I walk in multiple gifts, talents and God's word.

Twenty years later I married my soul mate. He's not perfect, neither am I but, we are perfect for each other.

We met while both of us were working second jobs. I was the librarian and he was the computer tech. We are both geeks. When I met him I thought he has to be one of the nicest guys I could ever meet. He made me laugh. He brought me chocolate and I would catch him just watching me walk by to put books away in the library. He still does it to this day.

He didn't like to shop so his clothes were basic to say the least. Years earlier I used to walk through the men's department in the department stores and say that I would buy my husband's clothes one day. I asked him on our third date did he like to shop. He said, no. I asked him gingerly if he didn't have the budget to shop or didn't know what to buy. He said," I have the money but, don't know what to buy". "Well, let's go shopping, I would love to help." I had the time of my life. Now, I know it is not clothes he likes to buy but, technology. His pastor said that my future husband was a diamond but, he was hid in a brown paper bag. He was right. Fortunately, God knew what was in that brown paper bag. He made, prepared and delivered that diamond directly to me.

I could utilize this entire book to tell how many heartaches, disappointments, hurt feelings, lies and embarrassment I have endured. Rest assured it all didn't all feel good but, worked for my good to get me to this point in my life. As I get older, I can say like Paul, "it was good that I was afflicted." Why? Because I can stand and appreciate God for all of the blessings He brought me. Now more than ever, I appreciate the courage, strength, wisdom and determination to move forward and live the abundant life He has ultimately given me.

    Who would have thought it? I am the least likely but, God.

Dr. Julia A. Royston
Author, Publisher Speaker, Songwriter
Jeffersonville, IN

"We love him, because he first loved us."
I John 4:19

What's Love Got to Do With It?

At 16 years old, I was already a statistic – another black, unwed, teen mother, and high school dropout. By the time I was 24, I had three children and was not married. I didn't intend to be such a disappointment to myself or other family members. I hadn't planned for my life to be this way. As a young girl, I'd dreamed of being married and having a family but, I got ahead of God. I was insecure and wanted to be loved. The void I felt was due to the fact that my family life was interrupted suddenly when I was a little girl, maybe four years old when my mother and father divorced. Although I was raised by my mother and step father until I was nearly 13, I never had the security that I had once known when my mother and father were together. Again, I found myself suddenly in a split from family life, my mother and step father were getting divorced and we were moving on again.

As I grew up, I tried to fill my insecurities in men that took advantage of me. Along with the fact that I was insecure because I was missing that fatherly love and protection, I was also tall and thought of myself as awkward. I was often picked on in elementary school. So those feelings added to my insecurities and feelings of rejection. However, as I grew older, guys started to take an interest in me. Not knowing how to handle the attention, I thought if I could just find someone to love me, we'd be together and eventually we could get married, have children and then I'd have that security that I was lacking and longed for. Instead of following the plan that God had for my life, I just went with the flow. The fact is, I couldn't follow God's plan because I had yet to know who God was. I didn't know yet how he loved me and he was the security I needed. I knew the name of Jesus and looking back, I can see that He loved me then, just as He loves me now. However, it would be years and heartaches later before I come to know him as I do today. I wound up a statistic, a broken unmarried teenage mother and high school dropout. A failure to myself.

I went through life the hard way. I struggled. I found myself in situations I didn't want to be in but didn't know how to get myself out of. I thank God that through it all, I didn't die while I was living a life of sin. I know even back then, He had His hands on me because, there is no way I should have been here today.

I would have to say it was destiny that brought my husband and me together and kept us together. Looking at both of our histories, there is no way we should have been getting married when we did. He was divorced and had two sons of his own. We'd been living together for four years before the Lord started sending people in our lives to begin planning seeds of faith. I had met a woman who had witnessed to me on the bus stop. She eventually invited me to her church and would constantly tell me to join the church. I invited him to come along and he did but, he was not wanting to commit to joining. Shortly after, he had run into a family friend who was a minister at a small church. My husband grew up in a family of ministers and friends of ministers. Christianity was very much a big part of his upbringing. The minister invited us to his church and we began to go there regularly. The minister would always let us know that it was wrong in God's eyes to live in sin as we had been doing. I became pregnant. This time, we decided to listen to the minister and got married.

Now we were married, had a family and were regular church goers. We thought were where ok.

But we fell into the trap that the enemy intends to put many believers in. We wanted to keep part of our lives to ourselves. We had not fully surrendered our whole lives to Christ. It was a said faith but not a total surrendering of all. Our marriage took many bumps and bruises. Whatever could go wrong in our marriage began to go wrong. We had all the troubles a lot of married couples go through such as: money issues, lack of communication, feelings of rejection, blame placing, fault finding and even infidelity. Clearly God's word gives us the freedom to leave the marriage if there was infidelity. But God's word also clearly states that God hates divorce. I loved my husband and I loved the Lord. It was during these trying times that I decided to hold on and allow God to fix what I had needed all of my life, me. As God would have it, these issues would come to the light, amongst other things. He would allow us to be pressed in order to get to the anointing that He placed in us. He'd also allow us to go through the fire so that we would come out as pure gold.

One of the many reasons why I didn't want to separate from my husband was my children. I knew in my heart that God was going to fix our issues if we just trusted and obeyed Him. I know people say that people should not stay married because of the children. To that I say, that's probably true for many but, I am a strong believer that the children should always be considered. I also knew what happened to me. My mother and father had very good intentions and more than likely very good reasons for divorcing one another. But their decision also had an effect on me. The same with my husband. His parent's decisions had an effect on him. I didn't want my children to have to move from home to house and watch me have relationship after relationship much like I endured as a child. I was not having that so again. I reminded God of His promises to me. I was determined to prove the devil to be a liar and God a promise keeper.

We tried to fix our own problems. Many times, we'd go through things without sharing or receiving counsel from our pastor or other elder's in the ministry. That was simply because we wanted to keep our sins hidden. We didn't want people to know what was going on in our lives. But God had to expose these issues and bring light to them because things were dark in our world. The only way out was through the light of God's word and His promises. The scriptures says 'For there is nothing hidden that will not be disclosed, and nothing concealed that will not be known or brought out into the open' (Luke 8:17). I was at a point where I didn't know what to do anymore but, God had plans for me. Plans to prosper me and give me a hope and a future (Jeremiah 29:11).

Love has everything to do with it

One afternoon, I spoke to my Aunt and I asked her to forgive me for something I had done. The words she spoke to me changed me from that moment on. **Forgiveness is yours already**.

My eyes were opened at that moment. I realized that I had not really forgiven my husband nor did I trust God for our marriage. I had too much pride to leave, and selfishly, I didn't want the shame of having to go through a divorce. I honestly didn't want my children to be in a broken home but, they would have been in a broken home anyway if I did not begin to truly trust God in all things. I began to realize that when Jesus forgave, he forgave selflessly. I needed to forgive. I needed to forgive my parents, forgive the people that used and abused me, forgive my husband and forgive myself. In doing so, I was freeing myself to receive God's forgiveness. It wasn't that God had not already forgiven me because he had. I was blocking myself from receiving His forgiveness by not fully forgiving others. I was holding on to things and not allowing God's grace and mercy and power to be released. God loves us so much that he forgave us for all of our sins. Even though we sin against him over and over again, he is faithful and just to forgive us because of **love**. So when someone asks, what does love have to do with it, you can answer with a resounding everything! I had to examine my heart and ask myself if I truly loved my husband. Not just the idea of having a husband and having a family. The bible speaks so poignantly about love. 1 Corinthians 13:4-7 says love is patient and kind. It does not envy, it does not boast, it is not proud it does not dishonor others, it is not self-seeking, it is not easily angered, it keeps no record of wrongs. Love does not delight in evil but rejoices with the truth. It always protects, always trusts, always hopes, and always perseveres. I decided to really love my husband as God loves me by applying God's biblical attributes of love towards him.

I forgave him and myself completely for all that we had done to one another. As I grew in Christ, I continued to learn the power of true forgiveness. 2 Corinthians 2:10-11, Paul says...'if there was anything to forgive-I have forgiven in the sight of Christ for your sake, in order that Satan might not outwit us. For we are not unaware of his schemes.'

His (Satan's) main goal is to get us to believe his lies and doubt God's promises. When there is doubt, there is lack of faith. I had to rededicate my life back to Christ but now with an understanding of his love for us.

It is during these times that the enemy gets mad and tries with everything he has to get you to doubt the love and promises of God. However, the only power the enemy has is the power of deception and it is only activated when you believe him. If we just simply walk by faith (In God) and not by sight (the carnal activities of this world, even our flesh), we would not be so easily deceived by him. I purposed in my heart to believe God. I refused to doubt God's word. Satan tried, and to this very day, still tries to get me to doubt God's promises. My husband and I have committed ourselves to God. We understand that we are mere flesh and that God instructs us to put no confidence in the flesh (each other) because man (flesh) will always let us down. Because we are so determined to trust God, the storms rage in our lives, the clouds many times hang low. We take long walks through the valley. But through it all, we have learned to lean not on our own understanding but in all of our ways to acknowledge God and let him direct our paths.

God has shown me how to work on me and how I am responsible for **my** actions and not to be concerned about my husband's. So I remained faithful, to God and my husband. I kept my vows to my husband because God kept his promises to me. If my husband decided to break them and leave the marriage, then that was his right and his free will. I decided I would love him enough to let him go if he so wanted. When I relinquished my self-righteousness and obeyed God's word, things began to change. I believe that my husband was sanctified by God, through my obedience, my chaste behavior and mild conversation (1Peter 3:1). But not only was he sanctified through my obedience to God, I too was sanctified through his. Not in my strength but in God's strength. God has proven himself to be faithful.

Peace That Surpasses All Understanding

It's been nearly 21 years. God has done exceedingly above and beyond what I had ever expected him to do. God has given us a love for each other that is unimaginable. We laugh together, we pray together and we respect each other. God removed us from the city that held so many distractions of outsiders. That in itself was a move of God. Just tonight, my son called me and said, "Mom, I long to have a wife so I can love her how dad loves you." He witnessed how things weren't always good but how we overcame the issues that we had. Oh what joy that floods my soul! When I think about what we have gone through and how we held the power to destroy this house that God built, I shiver at the thought. I don't worry nor am I fearful of infidelity, I have been completely delivered. I trust God. Not man but God. Every day, I find joy in watching my husband cry out to the Lord in worship. He wakes up early in the morning and prays over me while I am sleeping. He has found favor in the sight of the Lord. Through it all, I have learned to trust God. When we set our affections on things above, not on the things of the earth below, we can live in perfect peace.

The reason I am sharing my story with you is because I promised the Lord that I will sing of his mercies and I will confess of his goodness all the days of my life. This is my testimony and encouragement to you that with God, all things are possible, not easy but possible. It would have been easy to walk away from my marriage, the strength was in staying, trusting and believing and obeying God. Today we couldn't have more joy. We are each other's best friend. We've grown together and learned so much together. God promised that the latter would be greater, He is a promise keeper and that's just **part** of his virtue!

Epilogue

My journey may not be the same as yours but with assurance, I can tell you that you have to have a personal relationship with God and you must be able to hear clearly what he is telling you to do. I will never tell a woman to leave her husband if he is cheating or if he is abusive nor I will never tell her to stay. What I will say, which a woman of God once told me, fast and pray. Don't make any decisions until you hear clearly from God, and then be confident in where he leads you. If you trust God, don't let anyone else try to persuade you otherwise. God's thoughts are not like ours and he has a plan for you, a plan to prosper you and give you a hope and a future. God certainly has a plan for your life.

Tawanda M. Schultz
Recording Artist, Songwriter, Author
St. Louis, MO

www.ingramcontent.com/pod-product-compliance
Lightning Source LLC
Chambersburg PA
CBHW050639160426
43194CB00010B/1730